Original title:
A Blanket of Christmas Cheer

Copyright © 2024 Creative Arts Management OÜ
All rights reserved.

Author: Colin Leclair
ISBN HARDBACK: 978-9916-90-948-5
ISBN PAPERBACK: 978-9916-90-949-2

Fireside Wishes and Gleeful Moments

The flames dance while we gawk,
A marshmallow's fate comes with talk.
S'mores in hand, we cheer and grin,
Watch as the dog tries to drop in.

Hot cocoa spills on my new shirt,
Laughter erupts, oh what a flirt.
The cat climbs up for a cozy seat,
Dreaming of snacks and juicy meat.

Nurturing Notes of Love and Light

I wrote a note in cookie dough,
But baked it till it just won't show.
The sprinkles scattered, sweet surprise,
Love notes buried in a pie's rise.

I sent a message through the salad,
But giggles burst, it turned to ballad.
A heart-shaped crouton jumped with glee,
Now even lettuce loves you and me.

Celestial Whimsy and Snowy Delights

Snowflakes tumble with laughter clear,
As snowmen talk with mugs of beer.
They share their stories, quite profound,
While I just hope they don't fall down.

The sledding hill looks like a spree,
Kids bouncing off like they're on a spree.
Yet somehow manage to stay afloat,
While parents sip from their cozy coat.

Nurturing Notes of Love and Light

I wrote a note in cookie dough,
But baked it till it just won't show.
The sprinkles scattered, sweet surprise,
Love notes buried in a pie's rise.

I sent a message through the salad,
But giggles burst, it turned to ballad.
A heart-shaped crouton jumped with glee,
Now even lettuce loves you and me.

Celestial Whimsy and Snowy Delights

Snowflakes tumble with laughter clear,
As snowmen talk with mugs of beer.
They share their stories, quite profound,
While I just hope they don't fall down.

The sledding hill looks like a spree,
Kids bouncing off like they're on a spree.
Yet somehow manage to stay afloat,
While parents sip from their cozy coat.

The Spirit of Giving Wrapped in Wonder

I wrapped my presents with great flair,
But used my cat as my own chair.
Tape on paws, oh what a sight,
Now gift-wrapping's a furry fight.

The cards I wrote in messy ink,
Had doodles of penguins doing a wink.
In every line, a shared delight,
As elves giggle and take off at night.

A Season of Giving

With presents piled high on the floor,
A cat thinks it's a playground galore.
Wrapping paper, ribbons in a mess,
And Grandma's fruitcake? It's anyone's guess.

The lights twinkle bright on the tree,
But the dog thinks they're all for him, you see.
A season of giving, it's the thought that counts,
Especially when it comes to leftover amounts.

Warmth in Every Corner

Hot cocoa spills all over the couch,
As kids build a snowman with a grouchy slouch.
Blankets piled up, a cozy delight,
Except when someone hogs them all night!

Fireplace crackling, oh what a treat,
But the cat finds the warmest, juiciest seat.
Footed pajamas, a fashion so bold,
But watch out, or you'll get the fridge's cold.

Whimsical Winter Wonders

The snowflakes dance like ballerinas fly,
While squirrels conspire, plotting to try.
A snowball fight turns into a mess,
With more laughter than snowy success.

The jingle bells ring with a catchy new beat,
But the kids are just chasing after the treat.
Frosty the snowman with a carrot for pride,
Just wait until the dog takes it for a ride!

A Patchwork of Merry Memories

Grandpa's stories, oh what a delight,
About the time he flew a kite!
Mom's burnt cookies, a holiday cheer,
At least we know Santa won't be here!

Family photos with silly old grins,
And Uncle Joe's dance that always begins.
A patchwork of memories, stitched with a thread,
Full of laughter, love, and the things we've said.

Sugarplum Wishes

In the kitchen, pies are stacked,
A battle of crumbs, who's attacked?
Sugarplums dance in the night air,
I'm just here for snacks, I declare!

Cookies giggle, frosting hugs,
The cat's now wearing holiday bugs.
Sprinkled glitter, a festive view,
But why's the fruitcake still here too?

Laughter in the Chill

Snowflakes twirl like tiny dancers,
But I've lost my gloves—what a prancer!
Hot cocoa spills on my new coat,
And now I'm wearing a marshmallow boat!

Sledding down a frosty hill,
With pants so wet, it's quite the thrill.
Laughter echoes, cold noses red,
I swear I just saw a snowman spread!

Frosty Windows, Warm Hearts

Frosty windows, look at those shapes,
I see a reindeer with silly capes.
Hot soup spills, who made that chore?
Kitchen's a mess—there's more on the floor!

Snowball fights turn into a game,
But throwing snow at dad's so lame.
With cheeks aglow and laughter bright,
We'll chase the snow until the night!

The Melody of Holiday Whispers

Hushed whispers float on the chilly breeze,
But my aunt's gossip makes me sneeze.
Tinsel tangles, the lights all blink,
Is that a cat? Wait, what do you think?

Carols sung off-pitch and loud,
Our family talent—oh, so proud!
With eggnog spills and much to share,
This holiday joy beyond compare!

Rejoicing in the Snow

Snowflakes dancing, oh what a sight,
Slipping and sliding, not quite upright.
Snowmen grinning with carrot noses,
While dogs leap high in frosty poses.

Hot cocoa spills from mugs held tight,
As we race snowballs with pure delight.
The world is wrapped in a white embrace,
With cheeks as red as Santa's face.

Cherished Moments of Light

Twinkling lights on the tree so bright,
Cats in a tangle, what a funny sight.
Ornaments hang like an awkward crowd,
Each one a story, oh so loud.

Baking cookies, they vanish in air,
Flour on faces, we just don't care.
Laughter fills the kitchen, joy does spread,
Even the burnt ones, we eat instead.

Yuletide Reverie

Carols echo, off-key yet proud,
Singing together, we're far from cowed.
Mittens mismatched, we dance with glee,
Uncle Joe's jokes, as bad as can be.

Presents are wrapped in paper galore,
Finding the cat who's hiding for sure.
Under the table, he spies the treats,
Ripping the ribbons, he claims his feats.

Enchantment in Every Ornament

Each little bauble tells a tale,
Of last year's mishaps and epic fails.
Tinsel tangled in the dog's long hair,
Santa's hat now a fashion affair.

Counting the days with a playful cheer,
Our countdown clock is a little unclear.
With every giggle, our spirits ignite,
Joy fills our hearts on this magical night.

Celebrating the Glow of Togetherness

Gather 'round, don't be shy,
We've got snacks that can fly!
Chips that crunch, dips that swirl,
Laughter's the flag that we unfurl.

We dance like socks on a floor,
One step forward, two steps more!
With friends around, it's a blast,
Hold your drink tight, don't spill at last!

Board games stacked like a tower,
Who will claim the winning power?
In our chaos, joy's the key,
Togetherness is our decree!

Here's to mishaps that we adore,
Like spaghetti stuck to the door.
In every giggle, we find a glow,
That's how we celebrate, you know!

The Heartbeat of December

December knocks, it's a cheery guest,
Hot cocoa sips, we're feeling blessed.
Snowflakes dance on chilly air,
But watch out for bumpy stairs!

Lights twinkle like stars gone wild,
Every corner's a festive child.
Muffins baked with gingerbread,
Just enough to fill the spread!

Wrapping gifts like a clumsy pro,
At the end, it's one large bow!
Furry pets play with the scraps,
While we giggle through our laps.

The heartbeat quickens, what a scene,
With family quirks that reign supreme!
In every hug, a cozy embrace,
December, you're our favorite place!

Kindness in Every Snowflake

Snowflakes fall with gentle grace,
Each a smile, a warm embrace.
They tickle noses, chill the toes,
In winter's dance, kindness grows.

Catch a flake upon your tongue,
A tiny gift, so sweet and fun.
In frosty air, let laughter ring,
Kindness is the joy we bring.

A Festive Embrace

Tinsel shines on every tree,
Cats climb up it, oh woe is me!
The cookies vanish, all but crumbs,
And uncle Dave just drums and drums!

Lights that twinkle, hearts that sing,
Grab that fruitcake—what a fling!
With hugs so tight and smiles so bright,
A festive embrace makes all things right.

Tidings of Joy

Jingle bells and awkward socks,
The joy of laughter, it simply rocks!
Rooftops echo with festive cheer,
As aunties dance with too much beer.

Presents wrapped in paper neat,
Oh wait, there's cat hair—what a treat!
We toast to goodness, raise a glass,
With silly stories, the moments pass.

The Gift of Presence

A gift that can't be wrapped or tied,
It's laughter shared, with hearts opened wide.
No need for bows or shiny sparkles,
Just friends and fun, and maybe farcles.

In every hug and joyful cheer,
The gift of presence holds us near.
So let's embrace the silly dance,
And wrap this moment with our chance.

A Canvas of Cheer

The paintbrush slipped, oh what a day,
My masterpiece looks like a cat at play.
Colors splashed in a wild array,
I guess it's modern art, hip-hip-hooray!

With every stroke, my vision's unclear,
Did I paint a tree or a friendly deer?
My friends all laugh, they hold their beer,
Artistic genius? Nah, just a pioneer!

Holiday Emotions Unfurled

Tinsel tangled in my hair galore,
I danced too close to the kitchen door.
Cookies baking, I can't take much more,
The scale is yelling, 'Stop this indoor war!'

Uncle Joe's jokes, they just keep on coming,
Each punchline lands, my stomach's now humming.
The punch is spiked, and my head's now drumming,
Holiday cheer? More like holiday slumming!

Snow-dusted Happiness

Snowflakes falling, covering my shoe,
I slipped and slid like a seal in a zoo.
Build a snowman? I might give it a go,
But it'll end up looking like a lumpy dough.

Sledding down the hill, oh what a ride!
With a face full of snow, I'm filled with pride.
But when I crash, I'm full of despair,
Laughter echoes, but it's all in good care!

The Light in Our Hearts

We gather 'round, the fire's so bright,
Sharing tales of our silliest fright.
My cousin's story gave me quite the fright,
A cat in a costume? It's quite the sight!

With marshmallows ruined, we roar with glee,
My burnt snack? A masterpiece, you'll see!
As laughter takes flight, our spirits set free,
The light in our hearts, as bright as can be!

Warmth in the Winter Glow

Snowflakes dance and swirl with glee,
Hot cocoa spills, oh dear, oh me!
The fire crackles, popcorn's popped,
I sit here snug, my diet stopped.

Blankets piled in festive cheer,
I wear my socks - a sight, oh dear!
A snowman turned out quite a champ,
With carrot nose and veggie lamp.

The cat's now caught in yarn's embrace,
A tangled furball, what a race!
My mitten's lost, I laugh out loud,
In winter's grip, I'm snug and proud.

So raise a toast to winter's flair,
With jokes and laughs to share and share!
For warmth in chill is truly bright,
A cozy laugh on every night.

Twinkling Nights and Cozy Lights

The lights are strung all round the tree,
But tangled up? Just wait and see!
I'll climb a ladder, what a sight,
Our house now sparkles, oh, delight!

The neighbors peek through curtains tight,
As I trip over cords in the night.
With every bulb that brightly glows,
I wonder where the garland goes.

Hot cider spills, oh what a mess,
I claim it's art – no need to stress.
With twinkling nights so bold and bright,
Who needs perfection? Let's just light!

We'll laugh and sing, forget the fuss,
Can't find the words? Just giggle, thus!
With cozy lights and joyful cheer,
I'll raise a glass for all my dear!

Soft Whispers of Yuletide Joy

The stockings hung with little care,
Filled with goodies, and maybe hair!
I peek inside, oh what a treat,
A candy cane and socks – how sweet!

The tree spills glitter on the floor,
More sparkles here? I want some more!
Each ornament has a silly tale,
Like last year's cat that made it hail.

The cookies gone, the crumbs remain,
Was it Santa? Or the sugar train?
His laugh echoes from the night,
In every heart, he spreads delight.

So gather round, both young and old,
Let's share sweet stories, brave and bold.
With soft whispers of Yuletide glow,
Let joy and laughter overflow!

Embrace of the Frosty Evening

The frost is nipping at my nose,
As everyone piles on their clothes.
I step outside, the air so crisp,
A snowball fights with frosty wisp!

My face is bright, my cheeks are red,
Be careful there, don't lose your head!
I spin around, a frosty whirl,
And land face-first – what a swirl!

The icy sidewalks? Quite the game,
I'll glide along, oh what a fame!
With every slip, a laugh will ring,
For frosty evenings make me sing.

So let's embrace these chilly nights,
With warmth of friends and cold delights.
In every laugh and frosty call,
We heartily wish happy times to all!

Evergreen Dreams

In the forest, trees wear shades of green,
They dance and sway, quite the scene.
A squirrel wearing boots, so spry,
Asks me for nuts, oh my, oh my!

The pine cones whisper secrets old,
While winter's chill makes noses cold.
A rabbit hops with great delight,
Hiding treats for a hungry night.

With garlands made of last year's snacks,
The deer come by in little packs.
They nibble on the twinkling lights,
And start planning wild tree-frog fights!

Oh, dreams of evergreen abound,
In this magical, laughing ground.
With roots that spread and stories grand,
Nature's jester, oh so planned.

Hearth and Home Harmony

At the hearth, where stories bloom,
My cat is sure it's her own room.
With a flick of her tail, she claims the chair,
While I sip cocoa, without a care.

The oven's warm, a pie's on the rise,
But my dog just dreams of compromise.
He sniffs the air, his belly growls,
Staring at me with pleading howls.

Christmas lights tangled in a heap,
The kids are off, without a peep.
A tripping hazard, oh what a scene,
Guess we'll decorate next year's green!

Yet laughter echoes through the halls,
As family gathers, and joy befalls.
In this chaotic, cozy space,
We find our home, our happy place.

Festive Footprints

In the snowflakes, flurries swirl,
Tiny footprints make me twirl.
A snowman grins, his nose a carrot,
Waving at kids who come to share it!

They stomp around, a wild parade,
Chasing each other, unafraid.
With hats too big and mittens loose,
They tumble down like drunken moose!

Hot cocoa spills, a sweetness kind,
As marshmallows dance, so unconfined.
Arctic chums gather in a heap,
Sharing laughs, it's a giggly leap.

With footprints traced from here to there,
Festive fun fills winter air.
In this joyous, playful spree,
We make memories, wild and free!

Stars Above a Snowy Night

When the stars twinkle high and bright,
And the moon shines with all its might,
Snowflakes prance with a sparkling tune,
Making wishes, oh so full, like a balloon!

A penguin in shades, looking quite hip,
Slips on ice, does a double flip!
While rabbits race with a dash of flair,
They giggle and roll without a care.

The sky's a quilt of dreams so bold,
As secrets of winter gently unfold.
Each twinkle's a wink, a playful tease,
While the world below shivers with ease.

So let's gather 'round with a warm delight,
And dance 'neath the stars on this snowy night.
For every laugh and joyful cheer,
Marks the magic we hold so dear.

Wonders of the Frosted Dimension

In a land where ice cream is free,
And snowmen all dance with glee,
The penguins wear hats like kings,
While winter's melody gently sings.

A snowball fight with marshmallow fluff,
Our laughter echoes, never enough,
The icicles jingle like bells,
In this frosted land, all is swell.

Skiing squirrels race down the hill,
On candy canes, they find their thrill,
With gingerbread houses all around,
In this sweet world, joy is found.

So come take a trip to this place,
Where frosty wonders warm your face,
In the realm of the frozen delight,
We'll party till morning's first light.

Beneath the Boughs of Kindness

Under the boughs where the squirrels play,
They chatter and dance through the day,
With acorns stashed in their hats,
And a feast made of mushrooms and sprats.

Beneath the leaves, the rabbits hop,
With carrots they barter and swap,
A picnic spread just for fun,
With laughter ringing, their bellies run.

The raccoons sing a tune or two,
In a woodland cabaret, just for you,
While hedgehogs juggle tiny stones,
Their talent, no one ever disowns.

So come gather 'round in this grove,
Where kindness is the treasure we strove,
Let's share a song, a snack, some cheer,
With friends beneath the canopy here.

Flickering Flames and Gentle Peace

By the fire, where stories ignite,
And marshmallows roast till golden light,
The shadows dance on the cabin wall,
As we giggle and stumble, one and all.

The raccoon in pajamas snores loud,
While a campfire's crackle draws a crowd,
The tales of the spooky and thrills we seek,
With laughter that leaves us all a bit weak.

The stars above twinkle like charms,
While friends wrap 'round in warm, cozy arms,
In the glow of flames that flicker bright,
We find a calm in the heart of the night.

So here's to the memories we'll keep,
Where laughter lingers and fires leap,
In gentle peace, our worries cease,
With flickering flames, we've found our fleece.

A Symphony of Snowflakes and Cheer

Snowflakes waltz in the brisk winter air,
They tumble and twirl without a care,
With each flake a giggle, a twinkling sound,
A symphony formed with joy all around.

The cocoa is bubbling, the mugs are near,
With marshmallows floating like snowflakes dear,
We sit by the fire, sharing our dreams,
And counting snowflakes in sparkly beams.

Outside the window, the world's turned white,
A canvas of magic, pure and bright,
We bundle up tight, in layers we wear,
As laughter erupts in the frosty air.

So let's dance as the snowflakes come down,
In this cheerful land, we'll never frown,
A symphony played by the winter's own hand,
Together we laugh in this wonderland.

Magical Midwinter Nights

Snowflakes falling, a sight to see,
Fluffy friends frolicking with glee.
Hot cocoa spills, marshmallows afloat,
Every sip's a magical boat.

A jovial snowman, with a carrot nose,
He tells the best jokes, goodness knows.
With laughter echoing through the night,
We dance 'round the fire, oh what a sight!

Stars twinkle high, like disco lights,
As we sing songs 'til the morning bites.
A snowball fight? That's the best game,
Who knew winter could be so tame?

So grab your pals, let's light the way,
In Midwinter magic, we'll forever play.
With snowflakes twirling, spirits take flight,
These are the nights that feel just right!

The Dance of Joyful Spirits

In frosty air, they jig and spin,
Joyful spirits, the party begins!
With twinkling lights and merry cheer,
They dance like no one's ever near.

A tuxedo snowman, shuffling real fast,
High-stepping along, having a blast.
The festive music fills the air,
While winter critters join the affair.

With each frolic, giggles abound,
Creating laughter that knows no bound.
They twirl and glide through moonlit skies,
These joyful spirits, oh how they rise!

So if you're feeling a bit down low,
Just peek outside, let the fun flow.
Their dance will lift your heart so high,
Making winter dreams touch the sky!

Frosty Breezes, Warm Hearts

The frosty breeze whispers and howls,
As winter speaks, with chilly growls.
Yet inside, hearts are filled with cheer,
For warmth resides when friends are near.

Sipping tea beside a crackling fire,
With tales that never cease to inspire.
Laughter bounces, the shadows sway,
In cozy corners, we laugh and play.

Snowflakes tickle our chilly nose,
While a fireplace sings, it softly glows.
Bundled tight, we swap stories bold,
In frosty breezes, hearts turn to gold.

So as the winter chill takes its toll,
Let the warmth within keep you whole.
In every breath of frosty air,
Warm hearts remind us that love is rare!

The Comfort of Tradition

Traditions wrap us like a hug,
From fluffy socks to the holiday mug.
Every year, we cheer with delight,
As we gather 'round for our big feast night.

A table set with joy and care,
Grandma's recipes floating in the air.
With laughter and love served on each plate,
These moments, my friend, are truly great.

Decorating trees with quirky flair,
With tinsel that tangles in our hair.
Each ornament tells a tale of old,
A treasure chest of memories to hold.

So raise a glass to the funny quirks,
In the comfort of tradition, joy lurks.
Through every laugh and silly blunder,
We find our magic in winter's wonder!

The Enchanting Chill

The snowflakes dance like clumsy feet,
As winter's chill makes our noses greet.
We bundle up in layers so thick,
Yet still we find a way to slip and stick.

The hot cocoa spills on my brand new hat,
While squirrels eye my snacks, oh, imagine that!
The fire crackles with the warmth we seek,
But my cat steals my lap, and I can't speak.

Goblins in snowmen hats, they loom,
Using my shovel, they plot their doom.
With laughter echoing, oh what a thrill,
This winter tale, all wrapped in chill.

When igloos look like sad little huts,
And snow plows growl like winter's ruts,
We share our laughs, despite the freeze,
In this enchanted chill, we take our ease.

Cherished Carols

In the car, we sing with joy and glee,
Twisting our voices like a twisted tree.
Granny's off-key, but we all cheer loud,
With harmonies soaring, we feel so proud.

The lights are strung, but are they straight?
The dog thinks it's playtime—oh, what a fate!
Under the mistletoe, awkward we stand,
As Uncle Joe leans in for a hand.

Cookies in hand, we snicker and munch,
While Dad tries to carve the turkey for lunch.
Songs fill the air, with laughter shared,
In cherished carols, we're all quite impaired.

The spirit of joy, it fills the room,
With echoes of laughter, banishing gloom.
Together we sing, through thick and thin,
In this festive season, we all win.

Family Ties in the Frost

The snowball fight begins, it's on like dawn,
As cousin Timmy wears the snow as a yawn.
A winter wonderland turns into a brawl,
We dodge and weave, until someone takes a fall.

Mum's in the kitchen, her apron on tight,
Cookie trays groan, it's a glorious sight.
Dad tries to help but burns a few snacks,
While the dog waits patiently for the flax.

Grandpa tells tales of his frosty youth,
With tales so wild, we question their truth.
Family ties wrapped in ice and cheer,
A bundling of love that we hold so dear.

With blankets and cocoa, we gather 'round,
In the warmth of the laughter, our hearts are found.
Frosty outside, but inside we find,
Family ties that are sweetly entwined.

Serenity of Seasonal Love

The fireplace flickers with a cozy embrace,
As shadows dance in this magical place.
With candles aglow and laughter near,
The serenity of love whispers in the cheer.

Cards made of paper, with glitter and glue,
We create little wonders, just me and you.
Hot cocoa spills on our favorite floor,
With each sip we giggle, wanting more and more.

Outside it snows, a chilly display,
While we share stories that brighten the gray.
With blankets wrapped tight, no worry or strife,
This seasonal love is the joy of our life.

As carols echo through this tranquil night,
With laughter and warmth, everything feels right.
In the embrace of the cold, we still fit,
Finding serenity in the love we admit.

Jingle Bells and Velvet Hues

Jingle bells in velvet hues,
A cat in socks, with purring moos.
Santa stuck up the chimney wide,
At least he has a place to hide!

Elves that dance on sugar pies,
Giggles echo, oh what a prize!
Snowflakes fall like fumbled naps,
While hot cocoa's made in choco traps!

Carols sung by a penguin choir,
Softly wrapped in wool and fire.
Laughing at the reindeer's prance,
They tripped and fell in snowball dance!

Gifts that squeak and gifts that hum,
All I want is a bubblegum!
Jingle bells, oh what a cheer,
Next year, let's all disappear!

Memories Wrapped in Ribbons of Gold

Memories wrapped with ribbons bold,
Like grandma's cookies, warm and cold.
Laughter echoes down the hall,
As we trip on the cat's little ball.

Photos stuck with tape and glee,
Uncle Bob as a bumblebee!
A wig on a snowman stands tall,
Reminders of our funny fall.

Pine-scented candles flicker bright,
But they smell more like burnt delight.
Sister's face, a sight to see,
She's wrapped up like a Christmas tree!

Now we gather 'round with cheer,
To laugh and share our goofy year.
Let the wrapping paper fly,
For memories never say goodbye!

A Tapestry of Frosted Dreams

A tapestry of frosted dreams,
Crafted by playful snowy beams.
Hot cocoa spills, oh what a scene,
As marshmallows take their cushy bean!

Noses pink, and cheeks bright red,
The dog just snuck a Christmas bread.
Carrot noses for snowmen free,
But they become a meal for me!

Sledding trips with giggles loud,
While dad's face turns snowsuit proud.
Frosty fingers, frostier toes,
Into the hill, hilarity flows!

Through frozen air, we glide and skate,
But one wrong turn, and there's our fate!
Landing soft on snowflakes grand,
A frosty dream, but what a stand!

Frosty Breezes and Heartfelt Leases

Frosty breezes blow and tease,
With snowflakes dancing like a sneeze!
Neighbors grumble, shovels quake,
While kids make forts with icing flake!

Hot soup bubbles in a pot,
And grandma's hat? It's tied in a knot!
Chattering teeth and jumping feet,
As we dive for snowmen's retreat!

Heartfelt leases on winter's play,
Hoping for sunshine to lead the way.
Giggles echo, winter's delight,
The funniest show is our snowball fight!

So raise a cup of frosty cheer,
To moments shared, both far and near.
Laughter wraps us like a scarf,
In frosty breezes, we all laugh!

Hearthside Reflections

The fire crackles, oh what a sound,
As we ponder our snacks and the warmth all around.
Marshmallows toast as the flames leap high,
But who burned the cookies? Oh me, oh my!

We swap tales of trips and things that we've seen,
Like the time Aunt Sally danced in a dream.
Grandpa's snoring is louder than the flame,
Yet his tales are wild, never quite the same.

The cat jumps up, knocks the cocoa off,
And while we all laugh, Aunt Edna scoffs.
We'll get her a sweater to match her mad glare,
With kittens and rainbows—it's only fair!

So here's to the nights with friends all around,
Where laughter and love are the best things we've found.
We'll roast up good times, toast until late,
At hearthside reflections, it's never too late.

Radiance of Red and Green

Twinkling lights on the tree so bright,
Making our living room a dazzling sight.
The ornaments clash in a glorious mix,
Uncle Joe says, "This is my best bag of tricks!"

Gingerbread men stare with frosting delight,
While Aunt May's recipe shrunk overnight.
Every bite's magical, chewy and sweet,
But how did the dog manage to sneak a treat?

The stockings hang low, ready to burst,
With odd little gifts that can't quench our thirst.
A pair of socks with a reindeer on top,
Or a dancing cactus that won't ever stop!

Each year we gather, our hearts in a cheer,
To share belly laughs and good holiday cheer.
With red and green flashing, we're silly as can be,
In this joyful chaos, it's where we're all free.

Gathering Around the Fire

Gather around, let the stories unfold,
Of grand adventures, our hearts being bold.
Who caught the fish that was way too big?
Or who made the bean dip? We all want a gig!

With s'mores in hand, and bugs in our hair,
We joke and we laugh without a single care.
But watch for the sparks, they fly high in the dark,
Just like Grandma's tales, they always hit the mark!

The shadows dance funny on the canvas of night,
Later Keith's going to challenge the light.
To catch a firefly, he aims for the sky,
But stumbles and falls—oh my, oh my!

So cherish these moments, they come and they go,
The warmth of the fire, the sweet afterglow.
With friends by our side, we'll always aspire,
To gather our hearts around the fire.

The Glow of Evening Cheer

The sun dips low, paints the skies in cheer,
As laughter erupts, we all disappear.
To the backyard where stories come alive,
With a flashlight that flickers—oh how we thrive!

Neighbors peek over, they want to join in,
They bring their own snacks, a glorious win!
With popcorn and giggles, we all take a seat,
While Fred's karaoke brings rhythmic defeat.

The crickets chirp, adding beats to our night,
While we sing off-key, with all of our might.
The glow from the fire feels warm on our skin,
But you might want to check if your shoes are too thin!

So we toast to the evening, with spirits so clear,
Where stories and laughter fill up the atmosphere.
Here's to the glow, the warmth we all share,
In this evening cheer, we are free without care.

Fireside Memories

The logs are crackling, sparks arise,
Grandpa's snoring, what a surprise.
Hot cocoa spills on the dog's new bed,
A marshmallow monster, I think it's dead.

We roast our tales, both silly and bold,
The best ones told, we regale, retold.
S'mores stick to fingers, faces, and socks,
While shadows dance like jittery clocks.

The cat jumps high, as the flames jump low,
With so much laughter, time does not slow.
Fireside memories, forever they stay,
In our hearts, we'll keep them tucked away.

So gather 'round on this cozy night,
With friends and family, it feels so right.
Though jackets may be thick and hair may frizz,
We'll treasure these moments, just like this fizz.

The Warmth of Togetherness

In a room that glows, we laugh and cheer,
Sharing stories from yesteryear.
Mom's bad jokes, always a hit,
Dad's in the corner, can't handle it.

There's pie on the table, and crumbs on the floor,
'Till the dog starts woofing, we just can't ignore.
A game of charades, awkward but fun,
With lots of laughs, we can't be outdone.

So raise your glass to the warmth we share,
In this jolly season, with love in the air.
We cherish the silly, the hugs and the kisses,
For togetherness brings us the best of wishes.

As the night wears on, our laughter will soar,
With every hearty chuckle, we'll ask for more.
The warmth of togetherness, like a big, fuzzy sweater,
In this season of joy, nothing's better!

Holiday Threads

The tinsel hangs low, from the tree it sways,
Uncle Bob's sweater, it deserves some praise.
With colors so bright, it blinds the young,
We all pretend it's cool, 'cause it's just so fun.

The ornaments twinkle, like stars at night,
Each with a story, bringing pure delight.
Grandma's favorite, it's made of old foam,
Says it's a lesson, on why we call it home.

The holiday threads, woven with care,
Stitching our memories, none can compare.
With laughter and love, we'll decorate wide,
And in this strange sweater, we'll take it in stride.

So toast to the chaos, the fabric of life,
Embracing the weirdness, avoiding the strife.
For holiday threads, hold our hearts so tight,
In Grandma's old sweater, everything feels right.

A Season to Remember

The lights are aglow, and it feels like a show,
We sing off-key, but we put on a glow.
Eggnog spills everywhere, chaos we cheer,
Each laugh is a memory, each smile sincere.

From presents to carols, our spirits ignite,
With mischief and magic, it all feels so right.
Kids trap their uncles in snowball fights,
While parents debunk myths on long winter nights.

The season's a blanket, so warm and so tight,
With moments of mischief, pure holiday light.
We cherish the laughter, the games we create,
A season to remember, oh, isn't it great?

So gather your loved ones, hold them so near,
In each little mishap, we find our cheer.
The joy and the warmth, that's what we'll treasure,
A season to remember, a lifetime of pleasure.

Childlike Wonder

In a world where shadows play,
I chase my dreams, come what may.
I step in puddles, splash, and squeal,
With joy like candy, oh what a deal!

I see a cat that dares to dance,
It twirls and jumps; I take a chance.
I follow closely, giggling loud,
It leaps so proudly before the crowd.

I find a bug with sparkling wings,
It whispers secrets; oh, the joy it brings!
I crown it king of my backyard,
We taste the sunshine, no need for a guard!

With every laugh, the world expands,
In childlike wonder, life is grand.
So hand in hand, let's skip and run,
In this good world, we've just begun!

Cocoa and Kindness

With cocoa mugs, we gather 'round,
The frothy peaks, the sweetest found.
We share our dreams, our cookie plans,
While doing our quirky cocoa dance.

A sprinkle here, a swirl so nice,
We sip and spill like sugar mice.
With laughter flowing, warmth inside,
In this delicious, cozy ride.

Oh, sip your cocoa, taste that cheer,
A sprinkle of kindness, bring it near.
We lift our mugs, and dreams take flight,
Cheers to good friends, a sweet delight!

So let's spread joy with every pour,
In cocoa hugs, who could want more?
With laughter high and hearts so bright,
Together we shine like stars at night!

Glowing Moments

In the dark, a glowstick gleams,
I dance with shadows, living dreams.
Each flicker bright, a silly grin,
Like fireflies caught, let the fun begin!

I juggle socks, they fly and fall,
The colors clash; I laugh through it all.
With giggles loud, the floor is mine,
In glowing moments, I'll always shine!

A sprinkle here, a giggle there,
I twirl and spin without a care.
For every mishap, there's magic at play,
In glowing moments, we seize the day!

So raise a sock, let laughter soar,
In this wild dance, we want more!
With hearts aglow, and joy to keep,
Let's dance together, skip, and leap!

Beneath the Starlit Canopy

Under stars like popcorn tossed,
We lay on blankets, never lost.
We dream of worlds where giggles reign,
With every twinkle, joy's our gain.

The moon plays peek-a-boo so bright,
As we tell stories that stretch the night.
A dance with shadows, whispers low,
Under this canopy, let imagination flow!

With silly jokes and laughter rings,
We create worlds where our hearts take wing.
We catch the stardust, weave it tight,
Beneath this sky, our spirits ignite!

So here we lie, with wishes shared,
In childlike wonder, and none despaired.
With every giggle beneath the sky,
Together, forever, you and I!

Echoes of a Festive Hearth

The fire crackles with glee,
As marshmallows dance with tea.
Uncle Joe spills his drink,
We all burst out in sync.

The cat's got a festive hat,
Strolling like he's on the mat.
Grandma's telling ghostly tales,
While the turkey slightly fails.

Cousin Fred plays the old guitar,
Singing off-key, sounding bizarre.
A chair tips over with a bang,
And suddenly, a piano sang.

But time flows quick, like melted ice,
As laughter rolls like added spice.
We gather close, no gift required,
In love and joy, we're all inspired.

Candles in the Snow

Outside, the snowflakes pop,
As kids slide and land with a plop.
Candles flicker, soft and bright,
In the chilly winter night.

One candle leans, almost falls,
While toadstools watch it from their stalls.
A squirrel swipes a chocolate treat,
And waltzes off with hurried feet.

The neighbors hum a merry tune,
Joined by the the light of the moon.
All wrapped up, cozy and tight,
With cocoa dreams to last the night.

But just as we sip and glow,
Someone yells, "Hey, watch that snow!"
A snowball flies, chaos reigned,
And peace returns, a bit stained!

Twinkling Stars of December

The stars twinkle with all their might,
Whispering secrets in the night.
We're bundled up, but feeling bold,
Sharing stories, laughter, and cold.

A comet zooms past with a cheer,
"Wish on me!" it sings in our ear.
But oh my, what a silly sight,
Dad wishing for a one-horse flight.

Mom's over there, rolling her eyes,
As snowmen compete for grandest size.
"Mine's the best!" the little ones shout,
While the neighborhood gathers about.

But soon we're napping by the fire,
Dreams of warmth and holiday choir.
Stars wink down, keeping watch so clear,
As December wraps its charm near.

A Symphony of Snowflakes

Each snowflake plays a gentle tune,
Landing softly, a soft balloon.
They trip and tap on windowpanes,
Bringing laughter, with no refrains.

A snowman waves, slightly askew,
With a carrot nose that's lost its hue.
When the kids hop, jump, and glide,
A symphony of joy can't hide.

Yet one snowball whizzes by fast,
"Who threw that?" we giggle, aghast.
The snowflakes join in, swirling with grace,
As fluffy chaos takes over the space.

So gather 'round, let laughter dwell,
In this snowy, sweet, funny spell.
For in this shift of flakes and dreams,
Lies the love that forever beams.

Cradled by the Season's Spirit

In winter's chill, we all do play,
Wearing socks that seem to sway.
Hot cocoa spills, oh what a mess,
But laughter follows, nothing less!

The tree lights twinkle, all aglow,
As pets climb up to steal the show.
Ornaments fall with a clattering sound,
Our hearts still warm, joy knows no bounds!

With snowflakes falling, soft and white,
We ask, 'Is it wrong to have a bite?'
Cookies gone, the guilt is real,
But still, we smile and feel that zeal!

So here's to all the joys we share,
In every laugh and silly dare.
Cradled by warmth, we dance and sing,
Mirthful moments that the season brings!

Mirth Under the Mistletoe

Under mistletoe, we gather near,
With cheeky grins and plenty of cheer.
Tongue-tied folks and awkward shuffles,
Kisses stolen amid the chuckles!

A cousin's wink, an aunt's loud cheer,
Every tale told brings a merry tear.
Uncle Joe's dance, what a sight to see,
We laugh out loud, 'Who could that be?'

Cameras flash as we pose in glee,
A collage of joy, it's plain to see.
With holiday hats and silly wear,
It's pure delight, try not to stare!

So grab a sprig, join in the fun,
Under the mistletoe, there's love for everyone!
With giggles and hugs, our spirits grow,
Embracing the warmth, let the laughter flow!

Hearthside Dreams and Holiday Laughter

By the fire's glow, we gather 'round,
Tell tales of gnomes and lost socks found.
With marshmallows roasting, sweetness in air,
It's time to reminisce without a care!

The stockings stirred, a tinsel fight,
Who gets the last bite of fudge tonight?
With laughter bubbling and stories bold,
Every heart's a treasure trove of gold!

Distant carols drift from afar,
As neighbors sing, each voice a star.
With hearty laughs and playful shouts,
Winter's warmth is what life's about!

Chill or warmth, we won't decide,
With hearthside dreams, it's joy our guide.
So here's a toast, let merriment reign,
With holiday laughter, we'll never wane!

Radiant Dusk on Silver Snow

As dusk descends on silver snow,
We make snowmen, had to show!
With button eyes and scarves so bright,
They smile at us, a frosty delight!

Snowball fights in gleeful jest,
Who knew winter could be the best?
We tumble down the hill so steep,
With squeals of joy, we're wide awake!

As stars begin to dance above,
We cherish moments we dearly love.
With cups of cheer, the fire's warm glow,
Radiant laughs on the silver snow!

So raise a glass with family and friends,
Let the joy of the season never end!
With hearts aglow and spirits free,
We celebrate life, just you and me!

Threads of Joy in a Winter Quilt

In a quilt of chaos, stitches so bright,
Socks on my hands, what a silly sight!
I wrapped up my snacks, like treasures they've found,
Who knew winter fun could be frosty and round?

My cat on the couch, wrapped snug like a star,
Dreams of chasing yarn, oh, how bizarre!
He pounces at shadows, then naps with a sigh,
Winter's just cuddles, with a dash of a pie!

Snowmen are frowning, their buttons all mismatched,
But my carrot-nosed sculptor? He's quite the catch!
With a top hat that's crooked, he looks like a king,
Promising laughter, just let winter sing!

So here's to the winter, with its quirky delight,
Bundled in laughter, and snowball fights bright!
With friends all around, and cocoa in hand,
Let's weave our joys in this frosty land!

A Canvas of Kindness in Ice and Light

A canvas of kindness, splashed with some cheer,
In a winter wonderland, smiles up here!
Bunnies in mittens hop in a row,
Delivering giggles with each little throw!

While icicles dangle, like teeth of a beast,
Squirrels in scarves plan their snowball feast.
With laughter like snowflakes, they tumble and fall,
Painting bright moments, the best gift of all!

A snow angel flutters, with wings made of fun,
Spreading joy like confetti, oh what a run!
We dance with the flakes, and twirl 'neath the moon,
In a canvas of kindness, our hearts hum a tune!

So gather your friends, on this cold, cozy night,
We'll build dreams in the snow, as the stars shine bright.
With love woven thick, and sweet smiles in sight,
Our canvas of kindness makes winter just right!

Whispers of Winter Warmth

In whispers of winter, the tea kettle sings,
With marshmallows dancing, oh the joy it brings!
Socks mismatched, like a fashion faux pas,
Each step's a giggle, let's toast with a 'bravo!'

The fire crackles softly, a pop and a glow,
As stories unfold, and the laughter does flow.
The cat steals my seat, with a stretch and a purr,
While I'm left to ponder, does he know he's a blur?

Frosty the Snowman, he dreams of the day,
When winter turns warm, and the snow melts away.
But till then, he smiles with a carrot for a nose,
A cheerful companion, in his icy repose!

With whispers of warmth that tickle the night,
We gather together, hearts fluttering light.
In this quirky season, with love on display,
Let's relish the laughter that brightens our way!

Frost-kissed Joy

Frost-kissed joy dances on our frosty cheeks,
Snowflakes are winks, though winter feels bleak.
A penguin slides by in a mischievous race,
While I trip in the snow, oh, what a disgrace!

In mittens and hats, we venture outside,
Snowball ambush! Here comes my cousin, the bride!
With a whoosh and a laugh, her veil starts to fly,
"Don't you dare catch me, I'm too cute to die!"

Ice skating disaster, I spin like a top,
With each wobbly glide, I fear I will flop.
But giggles are golden in the chill of the air,
As friends tumble over, all frozen with flair!

So let's raise a toast, with hot cocoa galore,
Make memories and laughter, it's what we adore.
Frost-kissed joy surrounds us, a magical sight,
In this winter wonderland, everything feels right!

The Embrace of Holiday Lights

Strings of lights spark without a sound,
Twinkling and wobbling all around.
I tripped on a cord, oh what a sight!
They're laughing at me, this holiday night.

The dog is tangled, can't find his way,
Confused by the colors, he once loved to play.
The cat's in the tree, plotting a fall,
While lights flash like disco, we've had a ball!

Neighbors all peek through windows to see,
My holiday chaos, oh so carefree!
But in the mishap, we find our delight,
In the bright shining glow of this wild, fun night!

So here's to the laughter, the mess and the cheer,
With lights that may tangle, but bring us good cheer.
The embrace of the season, in laughter we bask,
This joyful display, a delightful task!

Mistletoe Magic

Under the mistletoe, I took a chance,
But Aunt Edna lunged—what a dance!
Kisses are great, a family affair,
But dodging the cheek pinch? Not quite fair!

The mistletoe's power is strong and wide,
It just won't let go, it's a holiday ride.
I thought I'd get lucky, but instead I got bailed,
When Grandpa shimmied in, oh how we all hailed!

In the corner I spotted a cousin so bold,
Under that green, he turned icy and cold.
The mistletoe magic, it's full of surprises,
And Uncle Joe's snoring? Quite the disguises!

So here's to the awkward, the giggles we share,
Mistletoe moments in strange places, beware!
With every sweet kiss, chaos crafts our fate,
This holiday magic—we're never too late!

Comfort Beneath the Wreath

Nestled beneath the grand leafy wreath,
I hit my head hard, oh how I seethe!
But comfort awakens, as I sip on cocoa,
With marshmallows dancing like a sweet little show!

The wreath's lovely scent, a blend of fresh pine,
Is it a holiday miracle or just a sip of wine?
Uncle Bob's trying to fix the TV remote,
Declaring it's broken—oh, what a quote!

Flames crackle softly, enhancing the mood,
Dad's telling old stories, they're really quite crude.
Yet laughter and warmth blanket all in sight,
Beneath that old wreath, everything feels right!

So, cheers to the comfort, the mess and the cheer,
In moments so bright that we hold ever dear.
With love wrapped around us in every sweet breath,
Together we sparkle, defying sweet death!

Joyful Hues of the Season

Red, green, and gold dance with delight,
Colors exploding like fireworks at night.
Every corner sparkles, a holiday show,
Amazed at the chaos that starts to grow!

My sweater is ugly, and so is my glee,
With candy canes hanging from every tree.
Snow starts to fall, making me slip—and slide,
While I chase after snowflakes, my face full of pride!

Joyful hues summon the laughter we need,
With cookies and candies, our every heart's greed.
As the carolers sing, off-key and loud,
We all join in chorus, feeling quite proud!

So here's to the season, the colors unbound,
In the joyful hues, our happiness found.
With friends and with family, we'll sing and we'll play,
In the warmth of our hearts, let the laughter hold sway!

A Tapestry of Yuletide Bliss

In a world of twinkling lights,
Socks hung with merry might,
A cat in the tree, what a sight!
Presents wrapped just too tight.

Grandma's fruitcake, oh what a treat,
One bite, and you might retreat,
Snowmen laugh, they feel the heat,
While children dance on their little feet.

Hot cocoa spills, marshmallows fly,
Elves at work, oh me, oh my!
Cheerful chaos swirling by,
'Tis the season, we can't deny!

So gather 'round, hear laughter near,
Belly shakers and holiday cheer,
In this blissful time of the year,
We toast with eggnog, don't forget the beer!

Glimmers of Frosted Dreams

Frosty breath, cold noses bright,
Snowball fights, quite a sight,
Slipping, sliding, oh what a fright,
But landing in snow feels just right.

Glistening lights twinkle and glow,
Neighbors peeking out, oh no!
Screaming kids like a wild rodeo,
Eggnog spills—who put on the show?

A reindeer shuffle, a clumsy dance,
Everybody's trying, take a chance,
But when Grandma spins, it's pure romance,
We all end up in a snowy trance.

With every laugh, our hearts expand,
Joy and giggles, oh isn't it grand?
Together in our frosted land,
Glimmers of joy hand in hand!

Wrapped in Togetherness

Cozy blankets, hot tea in hand,
Gathered around, our little band,
We tell tales that are quite unplanned,
Laughter bursts like a magic wand.

Mom's cookies smell like dreams come true,
But each one has a secret, who knew?
Some are burnt, a few are blue,
Still, we munch as if on cue!

A gift exchange with silly wraps,
Gag gifts hiding in playful traps,
Oh, look! Uncle Bob fell in his laps,
While grandma claims she's taking naps.

But through it all, our spirits rise,
In this chaos, we're truly wise,
Wrapped together like Christmas pies,
In laughter's warmth, our love supplies.

The Spirit of Giving

A jolly face with red-cheeked cheer,
With a sack of goodies, he draws near,
Kids making lists, what will appear?
The spirit of giving, loud and clear.

But oh! The woes of shopping spree,
Stuck in lines with an aching knee,
Wishing for gifts that are fancy-free,
In stores packed tighter than a bee.

Wrapping paper strewn all around,
With gift tags lost, how profound!
Some gifts received are truly renowned,
While others are just a weird mound.

Yet hearts are merry, spirits unbound,
With every smile, love will surround,
For in giving, true joy is found,
In this merry world, we are spellbound!

Joy in Every Corner

In the kitchen, cookies burn,
The dog is watching, can't discern.
We laugh as flour fills the air,
Joy's found in chaos everywhere.

A cat knocks over the tree,
Ornaments flying, oh what glee!
Uniting with family cheer,
Love's little mishaps, we hold dear.

Uncle Joe's dancing with no grace,
Partying like he's in a race.
With every joke, we can't stop grinning,
In our hearts, the joy is winning.

So let the mess be what it will,
These moments give our hearts a thrill.
In every corner, find a smile,
Joy's true essence, all the while.

Home for the Holidays

There's mistletoe hung in odd spots,
Great Aunt Edna tying up knots.
Cookies are hiding, oh the fight,
As we raid them, 'just one' feels right.

The cat is sprawled on the best chair,
Ignoring the gifts, without a care.
Family stories we retell with flair,
Each punchline lands with utmost dare.

The kids are bouncing round like balls,
Walls echo laughter, fun never stalls.
We wish it could last all year long,
With quirks and love, we belong.

Home for the holidays, it's clear,
Where chaos sparkles, joy draws near.
In every hug, the warmth we find,
In this absurdity, we unwind.

Luminous Winter Nights

Under stars, the snowflakes twirl,
With frosty breath, we all unfurl.
Sledding down hills, what a sight,
Laughter echoes through the night.

Hot cocoa spills down my shirt,
As I sing loudly—what a flirt!
The moon shines bright, a silver light,
Warmth in our hearts, feels so right.

The snowman grins with a carrot nose,
His stick arms flail, as if he knows.
In this icy wonderland, we play,
Creating memories that won't decay.

Wrapped in scarves and joy, we're tight,
Each moment's magic, pure delight.
Together we shine, like stars above,
In luminous winter nights, we fall in love.

Gathering of Hearthside Spirits

By the fire, the tales get big,
Old ghosts laugh, doing a jig.
With marshmallows roasting in the heat,
Spooky stories, our favorite treat.

Silly shadows dance on the wall,
Grandma swears she saw them crawl.
We scoff and giggle, hearts so light,
In this haven, all feels right.

The cider bubbles, sweet and bold,
While brothers argue over a mold.
With every sip, we toast the night,
To our spirits, may they take flight.

Gathering close, we share a cheer,
In this hearthside hub, we feel near.
For in laughter, love's magic spins,
A perfect recipe where joy begins.

Sledding Through the Starlit Air

Up the hill with sleds in tow,
We race down fast, oh what a show!
Snowflakes dance like they're on cue,
Screams of joy from me and you.

But wait! A bump, we start to fly,
Like Rudolph with a twinkle in his eye.
We crash into a snowman strong,
He tumbles down, but sang along!

With cheeks so red and spirits bright,
We ice skate by the moon's soft light.
Hot cocoa spills, oh what a mess,
But laughter's worth the frosty stress!

So let's sled on, through night's embrace,
With snowball fights, a friendly race!
In starry skies, our laughter glows,
Sledding dreams, wherever it goes.

Cocoa Kisses and Frosted Wishes

In a mug so warm and round,
Cocoa swirls and dreams abound.
Marshmallows plop like fluffy clouds,
In winter's chill, we laugh out loud.

Sipping slow, oh what a treat,
Chocolate sweetness feels so neat.
Frosted wishes float up high,
With every sip, I might just fly!

Whipped cream waves like fluffy cheer,
As friends gather, the end is near.
A snowball hits, oh what a splash,
But cocoa kisses make it flash!

With crazy hats and scarves so bright,
We clink our mugs, a wobbly sight.
Through frosty fun and cocoa bliss,
We share a hug, a warm sweet kiss.

The Glow of Generous Hearts

Lights are twinkling, spirits soar,
Cookies baked and fun galore.
Gift wrapping battles, awful tape,
Tagging 'From me'—oh what a shape!

Neighbors share their pie and cheer,
We gather 'round, the joy's sincere.
Passed along a pot of stew,
With flavors that could woo a zoo!

Advent calendars, hidden treats,
As laughter echoes through our streets.
Snowmen classier than me and you,
Decked in scarves, they shine anew!

With generous hearts, we fill the night,
In every home, there's love in sight.
Hand in hand, we laugh and play,
In this glow, we'd love to stay.

Tucked Beneath a Starry Sky

Tucked beneath the blankets warm,
We tell stories, share the charm.
The stars wink down with a twinkling glow,
As shadows dance and cool winds blow.

Hot cocoa dreams swirl through our heads,
As giggles rise from cozy beds.
Pillow fights and secret plans,
Imagining worlds where fun expands!

In this night, a blanket fort,
Our own kingdom, nothing short.
A dragon made of stuffed-up fluff,
In adventures, we can't get enough!

So here we snuggle, wild and free,
As winter wraps us tenderly.
Under stars, our laughter flies,
Tucked beneath a starry sky.

Tales of Frost and Fire

Frosty mornings make me shiver,
But a hot cocoa gives me vigor.
Snowballs fly, oh what a fight,
Laughter echoes, pure delight.

Christmas lights blink in the snow,
They put on quite the dazzling show.
But tangled wires make me frown,
As I dance like a silly clown.

The fireplace crackles, pops with cheer,
Let's roast marshmallows, grab a beer!
But watch the fire, don't get too close,
Or you might end up like a toasty roast.

So grab your friends, let's celebrate,
With jokes and laughter, it'll be great.
In tales of frost and fire we trust,
For joy and warmth are a must.

Stars, Snowflakes, and Smiles

Under the stars, we share a grin,
Wishing on wishes, let the fun begin.
Snowflakes fall and tickle your nose,
Laughing 'til we fall, that's how it goes.

With every snowflake, unique in its spin,
A snowman forms, let the games begin.
He'll wear my scarf, my hat too tight,
A fashion statement, now what a sight!

Stars up high twinkle in glee,
Can they see us? Oh, so carefree!
With hot chocolate, we'll toast tonight,
To stars, snowflakes, and smiles so bright!

So raise your mug, let's make a toast,
To laughter and love, we'll brag and boast.
With winter's joy, let's be awhile,
In the warmth of stars, snowflakes, and smiles.

The Warmth of Yuletide

The warmth of Yuletide fills the air,
With cookies baking, oh what a flair.
Santa's coming, or so they say,
Better be good, or hide away!

The tree is crooked, it leans just so,
With ornaments placed, and lights all aglow.
But if it falls down, what a laugh,
We'll just blame it on the cat's path!

Pine needles hug the floor like a rug,
While Aunt Edna's knitting gives a snug tug.
"Christmas is perfect!" she quips with pride,
As she loses her yarn, and it rolls outside!

So let's deck the halls with joy and cheer,
With family gathered, the season is here.
In the warmth of Yuletide, let memories beam,
Life is a frolic, a festive dream.

Together Under the Stars

Together under the stars so bright,
We'll share our stories, oh what a sight!
With blankets wrapped and cocoa near,
A perfect moment, spreading good cheer.

Fireflies dance as the night unfolds,
While ghosts of campfires tell their bold tales.
Laughter erupts as a joke hits the mark,
Holding our bellies, we kick off the dark.

The moon winks down, joining our fun,
We're all a bit silly, but oh, what a run!
"Who needs sleep?" we say with a grin,
While star-gazing dreams swirl out from within.

So here's to moments, both silly and sweet,
Together under stars, life's simplest treat.
With friends all around, it's pure magic we find,
In laughter and love, we're forever intertwined.

Echoes of Elves and Cheerful Chimes

In shadows of the woodland fair,
The elves are dancing without a care.
With bells that tinkle, laughter so bright,
They prank the squirrels, oh what a sight!

A snowman sneezes, twirls around,
His carrot nose flops on the ground.
The elves just giggle, oh so sly,
"Who knew snowmen could jump so high?"

With candy canes and marshmallow hats,
They ride on reindeer with silly spats.
A jolly dance in the moonlit frost,
In this winter wonder, no fun is lost!

So if you hear those cheerful chimes,
Just know it's elves and their silly rhymes.
They sprinkle joy in the crisp night air,
With giggles and chuckles, without a care!

Serendipity of the Winter Solstice

On the solstice night, when shadows creep,
A cat on a quest for fishy sleep.
His dreams of tuna dance in his head,
As snowflakes swirl like tales he's read.

The fire crackles, popcorn flies,
Mice in pajamas are stealing fries.
The cat pounces, but alas! He trips,
Into the punch bowl, swift little flips!

A jolly old man with a twinkle in his eye,
Sips cocoa while giving the cat a sigh.
"Bring me my cookies, my dear furry friend,
And I'll trade you for tales that never end!"

So raise a mug, let joy take flight,
In the winter's magic, everything feels right.
Let laughter echo on this chilly night,
As we dance through serendipity, hearts so light!

Lullabies Beneath the Evergreen

Beneath the pines, where giggles hum,
A hush of laughter, oh so fun.
The critters gather for bedtime stories,
With sleepy eyes and dreams of glories.

A hedgehog sings a lullaby sweet,
While fireflies dance on tiny feet.
Frogs leap lightly in the moon's glow,
As whispers of winter drift soft and slow.

The owl hoots wisdom from his perch,
While raccoons join in a cozy search.
For snacks and dreams, they softly sigh,
As starlight winks from the velvet sky.

So close your eyes, dear woodland friends,
In the evergreens where the magic blends.
With lullabies that twinkle and shine,
In these snug nights, every heart's divine!

The Magic in a Winter's Hush

In the still of night, the world takes pause,
A snowflake whispers, "Let's because!"
With giggles muffled and dreams to share,
The magic sings through the frosty air.

A bear in a hat sips steaming tea,
While penguins line up for a dance spree.
They hop on ice with elegance rare,
And slide on their bellies, without a care!

The tree tops sparkle with twinkling lights,
As owls share secrets of snowy nights.
A chorus of laughter fills the bright sky,
As winter enchants with a merry high.

So gather 'round, bring joy anew,
Under the moon's glow and tinsel hue.
For in this hush, our hearts will sway,
Embracing the magic of winter play!

Milton Keynes UK
Ingram Content Group UK Ltd.
UKHW022121091224
452185UK00010B/462

9 789916 909492